M000238985

Acknowledgements

To my tenderhearted and bearded husband Will: You have always believed in my voice. Thank you for encouraging me to write, even and especially on the days when I question my calling. Thank you for loving me enough to tell me when I'm not writing well. I can always count on you to tell me the truth because marital bias does not seem to affect your editing eye. Thank you for being strong when I am weak, for being smooth when I'm rough, and for being pliable when I'm stubborn. Above all, thank you for showing me how to make more room for Jesus. Your tender responsiveness to God's heart softens my spirit. I love you, Will.

To Tasha Burgoyne, Sandra Dragon, Cara Howard, and Cassandra Sanborn: Thank you for digesting my rough drafts and guiding me to better words and phrases. For this piece of work and all those in the past, you have handled my heart with care. Thank you for your wisdom, guidance, and technical expertise.

To Elizabeth Caudle: Thank you for lending your creative genius to this project. Thank you for being the kind friend I've needed in a season of change. You are consistent and steadfast, and your friendship has rooted me in many ways.

To Penelope: By the time this book is birthed into the world, you will have been birthed into ours. Before you were born, you planted a seed of hope in your mama's heart. You have softened me. I can't wait to watch you grow, to watch you find your voice, and to watch you continue planting seeds of hope.

To my Jesus: It has always been you. You are the healer of my heart, the companion of my days, and the savior of my life. I have no words without you. Thank you for loving this feisty, opinionated heart enough to never leave. I used to think I was too broken to be loved, but your love is drawn to my brokenness. I love you, Jesus. There is nothing better than being with you.

CONTENTS

Introduction

Christmas comes easy for some. We put up lights, wrap presents, and snuggle our loved ones close. Our cheeks are rosy with joy and our hearts are full. There are those who welcome merriment with little fuss.

Then there are the others.

There's you and me—the ones who trudge through the bristling winds of December feeling just as cold inside as it appears to be outside. We long for a jolly good time but something makes us feel not quite right. Many times, we feel just like an artificial Christmas tree – skimpy, fake, and see-through. So, we wrap ourselves in lights and disperse every ornament we can find, hoping their beauty will distract from our deficiencies.

I always forget about Advent until it begins breaking into my heart. I say breaking because that's exactly what it feels like. It feels like exposure and an uncovering of all my mess. My broken parts are laid bare. They cannot remain covered and dressed up when Advent comes knocking. It calls me out and asks, "What are you waiting for?"

The word "Advent" is derived from the Latin word adventus, which means "coming." This is a translation from the Greek word parousia, a fairly common word that can mean "presence." And if I'm honest, that's exactly what I'm waiting for—the presence of God. I don't want a temporary dose of Christmas spirit; I want pervasive, lasting joy that only comes when God shows up. Psalm 16:11 says, "In your presence there is fullness of joy." Fullness of joy can feel like a myth, but Psalm 16 makes it sound more like a promise.

I believe we have a choice.

Will we believe the promise that we have access to fullness of joy because of God's nearness? If so, then that's a promise worth waiting for.

In the Old Testament, God's presence is often preceded by an instruction for people to prepare themselves. Malachi 3:1 details the prophecy of one who would come to prepare the way for the Lord. Just before God delivers the Ten Commandments, he instructs Moses in Exodus 19:10-11 to prepare the Israelites for a divine encounter. In Leviticus 16 we read about the lengths at which priests had to prepare themselves before entering the Holy of Holies, the place where God dwelled in the temple. Over and over, we read about God's intent to be close to his people — a nearness that must always be primed by our preparation.

But you and I aren't living an Old Testament life. When Jesus ascended to heaven, he left us the Holy Spirit, which is the presence of God constantly in communion with us. There is no waiting on his presence because he is here with us in this moment. However, there is still something to be said for preparation. If we are waiting on God to do something in our lives, then we need to get our hearts ready. Whether you're waiting on fullness of joy or peace from anxiety or clarity in confusion, God wants to show up in your need. But you have to make space to meet with him.

Several years ago, I felt as if I was on the precipice of a God-sized shift. There was a stirring in my soul that whispered, "Get ready." I began having the same dream over and over for weeks. In the dream, God came to me gently saying, "Get your house in order." I couldn't shake the feeling that he was about to invade my life in a big way, and I needed to prepare myself for what was coming. As this feeling intensified, I knew exactly what God wanted when he urged me to get my house in order. For years, I carefully guarded a secret that had the power to ruin my life. Safely locked away in the confines of shame, I told no one. I immediately realized that if God wanted me to get my house in order, it meant uncovering the most painful part of my past.

One of my favorite stories in the Bible is found in John 5. It's the story of a man who has been sick for a very long time—38 years, to be exact. Jesus sees the man, but instead of immediately healing him (which he could've done), Jesus asks the guy a question: "Would you like to be healed?" The question sounds absurd. This man has been incapacitated for 38 years. Of course he wants to be healed! But then, suddenly, I hear Jesus asking me that very same question: "Maggie, do you want to be healed?"

This is the question that wouldn't leave me alone as I tried to get my house in order. The Holy Spirit began weighing down on me with persistence, "Maggie, do you want to be healed?"

Well, yes, of course, but I'm too afraid. What will people think of me? Will my husband leave me?

"But Maggie, do you want to be healed?"

It's not that simple, Jesus.

"Do you want to be healed?"

Jesus, the darkness is familiar, and the light is too vulnerable.

"My sweet girl, do you want to be healed?"

I finally said yes after months of wrestling. I remember the night I confessed my sin, stepped out into the light, and told the truth. My husband and I were sitting on our couch, and I sobbed as I told him that I had been lying for years. I was sure he would leave, but no amount of fear could defer the healing any longer. Do you know what my husband did? He put his arm around me and said, "Thank you for telling me the truth. That must have been so hard. I love you."

And just like that, I was free. Just like that, my house was in order.

On a quiet night in the most unassuming place, Jesus made a humble entrance that would change the course of history. Our great God in infant form did not demand royal fanfare at his arrival. He just needed room – room enough to be Immanuel, God with us.

So, if you're waiting on the Lord, I invite you to join me on this Advent journey, because it's time to get our houses in order. Let's prepare ourselves for a fresh encounter with Jesus. Let's clear out the chaos and clutter that have made their home in our hearts, and settle into the quiet tension that comes when we wait on God. Let's tear down the walls we've built up, and walk bravely toward the path of vulnerability. God will show up for us! *We need only to prepare him room.*

When He Shares the Plan

Isaiah 61:1-4

Reading

The Spirit of the Lord God is upon me, because the Lord has anointed me to bring good news to the poor; he has sent me to bind up the brokenhearted, to proclaim liberty to the captives, and the opening of the prison to those who are bound; to proclaim the year of the Lord's favor, and the day of vengeance of our God; to comfort all who mourn; to grant to those who mourn in Zion—to give them a beautiful headdress instead of ashes, the oil of gladness instead of mourning, the garment of praise instead of a faint spirit; that they may be called oaks of righteousness, the planting of the Lord, that he may be glorified. They shall build up the ancient ruins; they shall raise up the former devastations; they shall repair the ruined cities, the devastations of many generations.

Isaiah 61:1-4

Reflection

I became a follower of Jesus at a young age because I didn't want to go to hell. Once I reached adolescence, that motivation started to feel cheap, so I began asking Jesus, "How do you impact my life now?" I knew Jesus changed my destination, but I also wanted to know that he could change the journey. I needed to know my life counted for something other than waiting around to die and spend eternity without pain. Did Jesus care about the present hurt I was experiencing?

Isaiah 61 is a prophecy about what Jesus came to do. Jesus even shared his rescue plan by quoting this prophecy in the Nazarean synagogue in Luke 4:17-21. He came to save us from sin and usher us into eternity with the Father, but he also came to heal our broken hearts and to set us free from bondage and to give us a new song to sing. And it doesn't end there! Jesus was never planning to do this alone. Isaiah 61:3-4 lets us in something vital—we get to be part of the action! We are the oaks of righteousness who have been planted by the Lord so that he may be glorified. We will build up the ancient ruins. We will raise up the former devastations and repair spaces that have been ruined for generations. We get to be part of the healing work! This changes everything.

The account of Jesus' ascension is found in Acts 1. After their Lord disappeared, the disciples stood staring at the sky.

As the disciples stood with gaping mouths and strained eyes, two white-robed men appeared and said, "Why are you standing there staring into heaven?" The next account we read of the disciples details them in community and on mission. They stopped staring at the sky and got to work.

Where is Jesus calling you to join him on mission? What ancient ruin will you rebuild? What devastated place will you restore? Being a follower of Jesus is just that—it's following him into hard places instead of staring at the sky.

When He Rewrites Your Story

Matthew 1:1-16

Reading

This is a record of the ancestors of Jesus the Messiah, a descendant of David and of Abraham: Abraham was the father of Isaac. Isaac was the father of Jacob. Jacob was the father of Judah and his brothers.

Judah was the father of Perez and Zerah (whose mother was Tamar). Perez was the father of Hezron. Hezron was the father of Ram. Ram was the father of Amminadab. Amminadab was the father of Nahshon. Nahshon was the father of Salmon. Salmon was the father of Boaz (whose mother was Rahab).

Boaz was the father of Obed (whose mother was Ruth). Obed was the father of Jesse. Jesse was the father of King David. David was the father of Solomon (whose mother was Bathsheba, the widow of Uriah). Solomon was the father of Rehoboam. Rehoboam was the father of Abijah. Abijah was the father of Asa.

Asa was the father of Jehoshaphat. Jehoshaphat was the father of Jehoram. Jehoram was the father of Uzziah. Uzziah was the father of Jotham. Jotham was the father of Ahaz. Ahaz was the father of Hezekiah. Hezekiah was the father of Manasseh. Manasseh was the father of Amon. Amon was the father of Josiah. Josiah was the father of Jehoiachin and his brothers (born at the time of the exile to Babylon).

After the Babylonian exile: Jehoiachin was the father of Shealtiel. Shealtiel was the father of Zerubbabel. Zerubbabel was the father of Abiud. Abiud was the father of Eliakim. Eliakim was the father of Azor. Azor was the father of Zadok. Zadok was the father of Akim.

Akim was the father of Eliud. Eliud was the father of Eleazar. Eleazar was the father of Matthan. Matthan was the father of Jacob. Jacob was the father of Joseph, the husband of Mary. Mary gave birth to Jesus, who is called the Messiah.

Matthew 1:1-16

Reflection

We all come to the table with a story, a culmination of days and weeks that begin to shape who we are and how we see the world. It's easy to craft an image of God based on our life circumstances. If you had an abusive dad, then God is an authoritarian father just waiting for you to fail. If you grew up poor, then God can seem stingy and withholding. If you had an absent parent, then God can easily feel distant and uncaring. The truth is that our past shapes our perspective. But Jesus is in the business of making things new. He wants to rewrite your story and reframe your perspective.

At first glance, the book of Matthew begins with a boring list of biblical names that are hard to pronounce. However, Scripture tends to insert glorious treasure in seemingly mundane settings, which is exactly what happens in Matthew 1. There are five women mentioned in the genealogy of Jesus, which would have been scandalous to the intended Jewish reader. Women were never listed in genealogies! Not only was their presence outrageous, but the women Matthew chose to highlight were deplorable. Tamar seduces her father-in-law to get pregnant in Genesis 38, Rahab is described as a prostitute in Joshua 2, Ruth is a Moabite whose family history began with incest in Genesis 19, Bathsheba was the woman who held King David's adulterous affections in 2 Samuel 11, and Mary was an unwed, pregnant teen. These are the women Matthew included when introducing us to Jesus for the very first time. By including these five names, Matthew swings wide the doors of grace. There is not one who is too despicable to be in the company of Jesus. There is not one story that is past the point of redemption.

Jesus has the power to rewrite your story and he wants to repurpose your pain for joy. Will you let him? What messy or painful parts of your story do you need to bring to Jesus in prayer? No parts of our stories are wasted in his hands.

When He Keeps His Promise

Hebrews 8:6

Reading

But now Jesus, our High Priest, has been given a ministry that is far superior to the old priesthood, for he is the one who mediates for us a far better covenant with God, based on better promise.

Hebrews 8:6

Reflection

My mama always says, "Rules without relationship equals rebellion." I think that's why Jesus became our High Priest. We had no access to the Father before Jesus. Religion was a regiment of rules instead of an invitation to grace, but then Jesus entered the scene. Rules never have the power to redeem; only relationship can do that. Jesus rewrote the script so that reconciliation became our reality. No more measuring, no more counting, and no more weighing. There's a better way.

Jesus doesn't tell us to pull ourselves up by our bootstraps and he won't urge you to suck it up. He draws near to those who don't measure up. In Matthew 11:29-30, Jesus says, "Take my yoke upon you. Let me teach you, because I am humble and gentle at heart, and you will find rest for your souls. For my yoke is easy to bear, and the burden I give you is light."

There are two kinds of yokes: the yoke of slavery and the yoke of freedom. We get to choose which one we pick up. The yoke of slavery is full of weighty rules that never end. Jesus promised that the yoke of freedom would be better, lighter, and sweeter. There's one thing I know: Jesus keeps his word. In what way does freedom change how you live your life?

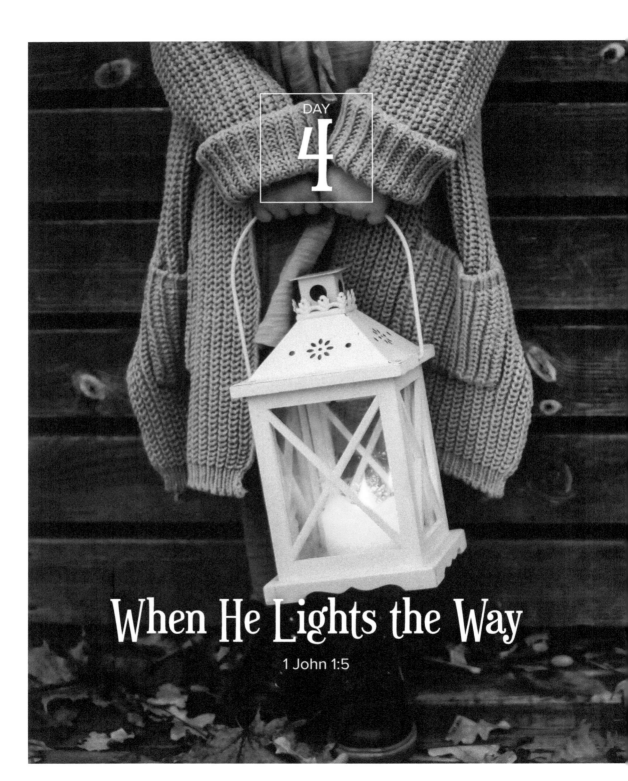

When He Lights the Way

1 John 1:5

Reading

This is the message we heard from Jesus and now declare to you: God is light, and there is no darkness in him at all.

1 John 1:5

Reflection

I've always been afraid of the dark. It's why I don't like playing laser tag or living in the country. It's also why I keep a nightlight on while sleeping even though I'm a grown, adult woman. There's something about darkness that feels unsafe and crippling. I know my fear is illogical, but paranoia has never been friends with reason. The day I read 1 John 1:5 was the best day of my life. God is the opposite of everything I fear! He is secure, he is good, he is kind, and most importantly, he is light. There is no crack or crevice that can remain hidden when God shows up. Life with him means life in the light. That sounded wonderful to me until I realized the implications. It meant no more hiding.

From the beginning pages of our story with God, we mastered the art of hiding. We cover up the parts of ourselves that we deem unworthy or useless. We tuck them away and present a polished, partial version of ourselves. The tragedy is that God's power is most evident in the parts we push to the side.

I don't like it, but it's Good News for the parts of myself that are hidden from view—the unfettered rage, the suspicion, and the anxiety. Bringing the mess of our lives into the light allows us to believe the truth about who God says we are.

Have you been hunkered down in hiding? It's time to walk in the light. In what way can you take a step out of hiding and into the light today? The first step might be scary, but the warmth of freedom is worth the risk.

DAY

5

When He Comes to the Wilderness

Isaiah 40:3-5

Reading

Listen! It's the voice of someone shouting,
"Clear the way through the wilderness for the Lord!
Make a straight highway through the wasteland for our God!
Fill in the valleys and level the mountains and hills.
Straighten the curves, and smooth out the rough places.
Then the glory of the Lord will be revealed, and all people will see it together.
The Lord has spoken!"

Isaiah 40:3-5

Reflection

My parents got divorced when I was a sophomore in college. Their marriage had always been tense at best and volatile at worst, so their split did not come as a surprise to me. Even still, the news felt like a gut punch as I found myself paralyzed by the finality of it all. As fate—or God—would have it, I was rushed to the emergency room for an unexpected surgery just days after learning of my parents' separation. Within one week, I was on a plane home to spend the rest of the semester in physical recovery, all the while surrounded by tumultuous family relationships and dysfunction. I've never felt more alone than I did in that season.

There's something about the wilderness that unveils the truth about our hearts. The wilderness is where spiritual platitudes fade away and all that remains is raw honesty. It was excruciating as I came face-to-face with the darkest parts of myself. I longed to feel God's presence instead of overwhelming rage and bitterness.

Imagine the Israelites in exile reading Isaiah 40 and wondering when God would bring them back home. The prophet commands the people to prepare for the Lord's coming even while they're still in the wilderness. The geographical words used in this passage are meant to reflect spiritual preparation. The landless Israelites knew they had no control over valleys and mountains and hills, but they had control over their own hearts. In this proclamation, the prophet is appealing to exodus imagery, and the people would have undoubtedly remembered God coming to them in the wilderness from the top of Mount Sinai. The prophet was calling for a new kind of exodus, one where God would once again meet them in the wilderness.

God's presence requires our preparation. Are there crooked places in your life that need to be made straight? Is there a roughness in your heart that needs to be smoothed over? God can meet you wherever you are, but imagine the outcome if you were ready for him.

When He Brings Healing

Hosea 6:1-3

Reading

"Come, let us return to the Lord. He has torn us to
pieces; now he will heal us. He has injured us; now he
will bandage our wounds. In just a short time he will
restore us, so that we may live in his presence. Oh, that
we might know the Lord! Let us press on to know him.
He will respond to us as surely as the arrival of dawn or
the coming of rains in early spring."

Hosea 6:1-3

Reflection

C.S. Lewis was a master storyteller who wrote about the kingdom of God, sometimes subtly and others times overtly. In The Voyage of the Dawn Treader, Eustace, an annoying and pretentious boy, gets turned into a dragon as a manifestation of the selfishness that resides in his heart. After much soul-searching, Eustace tries to tear off his dragon skin so he can be a boy again. No matter how hard he tries, the dragon skin will not come off.

"You will have to let me undress you," says Aslan the Lion.
Eustace was desperate by this point. Aslan had sharp claws that would undoubtedly cause severe pain, but Eustace agreed to let him peel off the dragon skin anyway. Aslan was his only hope. This is what happens:

"The very first tear he made was so deep that I thought it had gone right into my heart. And when he began pulling the skin off, it hurt worse than anything I've ever felt. The only thing that made me able to bear it was just the pleasure of feeling the stuff peel off.

Well, he peeled the beastly stuff right off—just as I thought I'd done it myself the other three times, only they hadn't hurt—and there it was lying on the grass: only ever so much thicker, and darker, and more knobbly-looking than the others had been. And there was I as smooth and soft as a peeled switch and smaller than I had been. Then he caught hold of me—I didn't like that much for I was very tender underneath now that I'd no skin on—and he threw me into the water. It smarted like anything only for a moment. After that it became perfectly delicious and as soon as I started swimming and splashing I found that all the pain had gone from my arm. And then I saw why. I'd turned into a boy again...

After a bit the lion took me out and dressed me...in new clothes."

We are Eustace. Our hearts are hard and our pride is strong, but Jesus heals those who return to him. Our God is not aloof and unconcerned with our need. Instead he is attentive and responsive when we call out. He is the only one who is strong enough to bring healing. We can't rip off the scales on our own; Jesus must do it. Will you trust him to heal you?

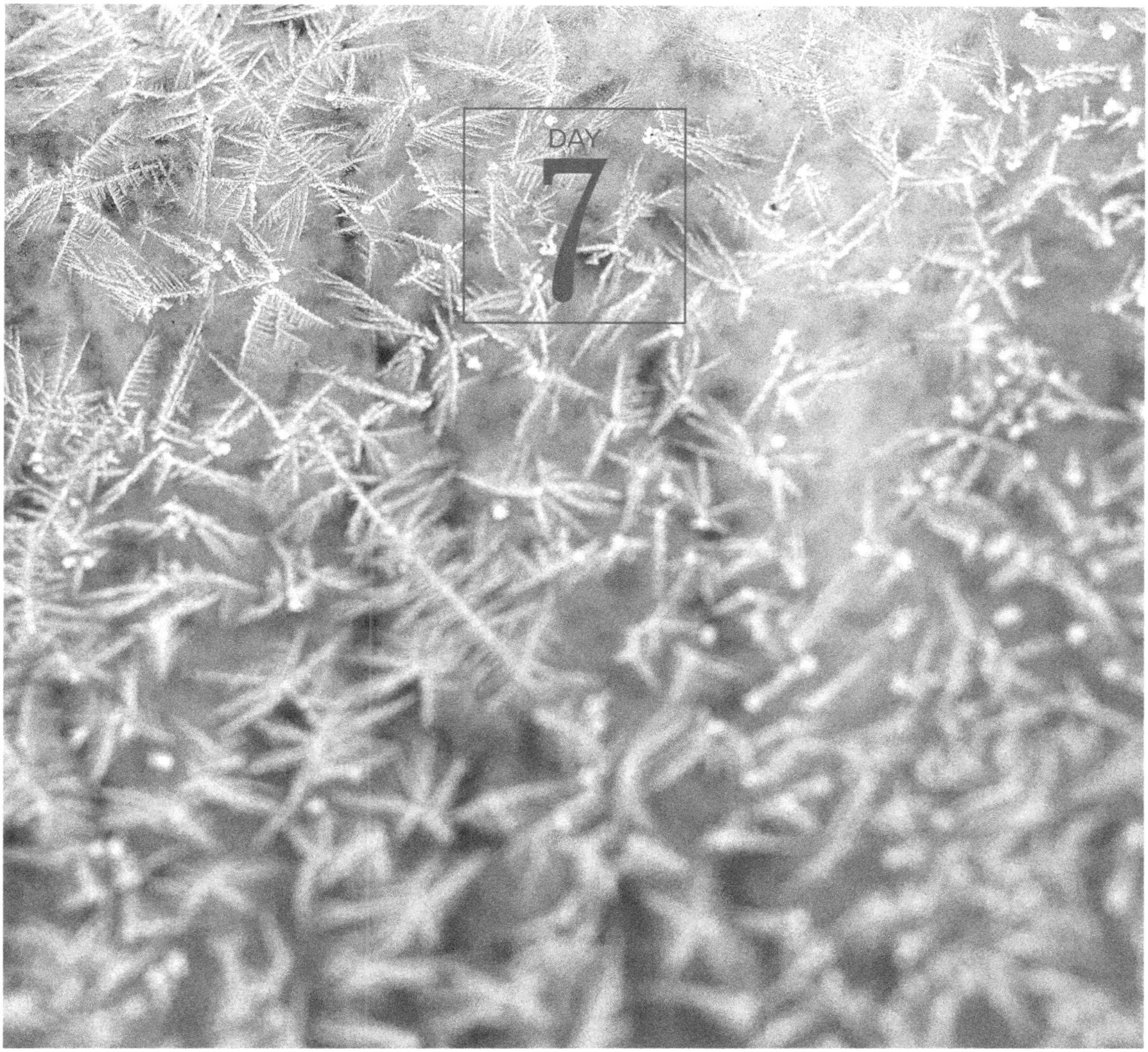

When He Forgives

Psalm 32:1-5

Reading

Oh, what joy for those whose disobedience is forgiven, whose sin is put out of sight! Yes, what joy for those whose record the Lord has cleared of guilt, whose lives are lived in complete honesty! When I refused to confess my sin, my body wasted away, and I groaned all day long. Day and night your hand of discipline was heavy on me. My strength evaporated like water in the summer heat. Finally, I confessed all my sins to you and stopped trying to hide my guilt. I said to myself, "I will confess my rebellion to the Lord." And you forgave me! All my guilt is gone.

Psalm 32:1-5

Reflection

King David had quite the reputation in Israel. He was courageous, creative, and compassionate, but even the best kings are prone to wander. David's biggest failure is widely known as his affair with Bathsheba, a scandal he tried to cover up repeatedly. The prophet Nathan confronts David about his sin in 2 Samuel 12, and David responds in repentance and sorrow. So, when David wrote Psalm 32, I think he knew a little something about the joy of forgiveness. He was familiar with the weight that comes when we hide our sin and the freedom that confession brings.

In verse 2, David says that there is joy for those whose lives are lived in total honesty. The Hebrew word for "lives" in this verse is ruakh, which can also be translated "spirit." It's meant to describe the intangible part of a person that goes beyond flesh and blood. Is my spirit laid bare before God? My outward life can appear honest while my inward life hides in deceit, but God wants all of me. He wants all of you, too. There is freedom when we bring our whole selves into communion with him. The enemy tries to convince us that confession isn't worth the risk, but that's a sack of lies. Joy is our inheritance, and it's time to take hold of what belongs to us through Jesus Christ.

God longs to forgive, but he can't forgive what we refuse to confess. He can't take the burdens that we cling to. Joy is just around the corner. All we have to do is confess; God will handle the rest. Is there an area of your life that you've been trying to hide from God? What do you need to confess today?

DAY

8

When He Transforms Us

Ezekiel 11:18-20

Reading

"When the people return to their homeland, they will remove every trace of their vile images and detestable idols. 19 And I will give them singleness of heart and put a new spirit within them. I will take away their stony, stubborn heart and give them a tender, responsive heart, 20 so they will obey my decrees and regulations. Then they will truly be my people, and I will be their God."

Ezekiel 11:18-20

Reflection

We know something is important to God when it's repeated in Scripture. The words in Ezekiel 11:18-20 can also be found in Ezekiel 36:26-27, as if someone copied and pasted the thought. That is God's way of saying, "Pay attention! I'm telling you something important!" When the Israelites were in exile, they were introduced to pagan gods and some began to engage in idol worship, forsaking their love for Yahweh alone. In his mercy, God promised to restore them to their land but also to himself. He promised to give them hearts that would no longer be divided in devotion but that were firmly fixed on his covenant love.

I resonate with the Israelites in this passage, because my heart has often felt stony and stubborn. My temperament is unequivocally rebellious. If I'm told to do one thing, then I immediately want to do the opposite. The stronger the command, the harder my resistance, yet I long for God to replace my stony stubbornness with tender obedience.

In what area of your life is God calling you to be more responsive in obedience? Ask him to remove any idols that have burrowed their way into your heart. Whether it's status or security or video games or chocolate, nothing can stand between God and his love for you.

When He Was Tempted

Luke 4:1-13

Reading

Then Jesus, full of the Holy Spirit, returned from the Jordan River. He was led by the Spirit in the wilderness, where he was tempted by the devil for forty days. Jesus ate nothing all that time and became very hungry. Then the devil said to him, "If you are the Son of God, tell this stone to become a loaf of bread." But Jesus told him, "No! The Scriptures say, 'People do not live by bread alone.'" Then the devil took him up and revealed to him all the kingdoms of the world in a moment of time. "I will give you the glory of these kingdoms and authority over them," the devil said, "because they are mine to give to anyone I please. I will give it all to you if you will worship me." Jesus replied, "The Scriptures say, 'You must worship the Lord your God and serve only him.'" Then the devil took him to Jerusalem, to the highest point of the Temple, and said, "If you are the Son of God, jump off! 10 For the Scriptures say, 'He will order his angels to protect and guard you. And they will hold you up with their hands so you won't even hurt your foot on a stone.'" Jesus responded, "The Scriptures also say, 'You must not test the Lord your God.'" When the devil had finished tempting Jesus, he left him until the next opportunity came.

Luke 4:1-13

Reflection

I've always been a runner. In high school, my dad helped me train for cross country and track meets. At a certain point in my training, I'd look at him and whine, "I'm tired!" This complaint never brought the reprieve I hoped for. Instead, he would retort back, "You get in shape when you run while you're tired." As much as I hate to admit it, he was right.

Jesus showed us that the same is true when it comes to our spiritual lives. He was led by the Spirit into the wilderness where he ate nothing for 40 days. That's 39 and a half days longer than it takes for me to get hangry. That 40-day time span is when the devil began to tempt Jesus. It's interesting to note Jesus's response after each one of Satan's attempts. The Messiah quoted Scripture. He didn't reason with Satan, and he didn't try to talk his way out of the temptations. His responses were immediate and succinct: "The Scriptures say..."

Right after this account, Luke writes in verse 14, "Then Jesus returned to Galilee, filled with the Holy Spirit's power." You get in shape when you run while you're tired.

The enemy is looking for your weak points, but it's a lot easier to resist temptation when we know what's true. Like Jesus, let's not allow temptation to become a discussion. What passage of Scripture can you meditate on today to remind you of what's true? Truth helps us keep running even when we're tired.

When He Prioritizes Reconciliation

Matthew 5:23-24

Reading

"So if you are presenting a sacrifice at the altar in the Temple and you suddenly remember that someone has something against you, leave your sacrifice there at the altar. Go and be reconciled to that person. Then come and offer your sacrifice to God."

Matthew 5:23-24

Reflection

The Sermon on the Mount is one of Jesus's most famous teachings in the New Testament. It's where he flips the law on its head and gives us a new understanding of righteousness. Jesus wants us to know what life looks like in his kingdom, and Matthew 5 is where he begins laying out the practical applications. He talks about things like loving your enemy and being a light to the world. He tells us to be peacemakers, and that hating someone is akin to murdering them in our hearts. Immediately after his teaching about anger and murder comes our reading for today.

Verse 23 begins with the word "so," or "therefore" in other translations. This word gives us a hint to look back to previous verses for context. When Jesus tells us that anger and hatred of another person endangers our souls, he is setting us up to take his next command seriously. Since despising another person puts our souls at risk, it is unlikely that God would accept our worship while we're harboring hatred in our hearts. But that's not exactly what our passage says, is it? Read verse 23 again. If you remember that someone has something against you, leave your sacrifice at the altar. Here's the rub: am I responsible for someone else's grudge against me?

Let's rewind all the way back to Matthew 5:9 where Jesus says, "God blesses those who work for peace, for they will be called children of God." What does it mean to be a child of God? It means we work for peace, even if the lack thereof did not begin with us. This is the hard work of reconciliation that Jesus models for us. He initiated a rescue plan for people who despised him. He died for people who wanted him dead.

Jesus is calling you to follow in his footsteps and choose the path of reconciliation. It doesn't matter where the hatred started; let peace begin with you. How can you work for peace today? Is there a grudge you need to lay down? Is there a broken relationship that needs to be addressed? Pray for God's grace to pursue reconciliation and take a step toward peace.

DAY
11

When He Creates Community

Colossians 3:15-17

Reading

And let the peace that comes from Christ rule in your hearts. For as members of one body you are called to live in peace. And always be thankful. Let the message about Christ, in all its richness, fill your lives. Teach and counsel each other with all the wisdom he gives. Sing psalms and hymns and spiritual songs to God with thankful hearts. And whatever you do or say, do it as a representative of the Lord Jesus, giving thanks through him to God the Father.

Colossians 3:15-17

Reflection

For as long as I can remember, it's been important for me to cultivate my personal relationship with Jesus. There is intimacy in the quiet moments when I commune with him that I will always cherish. But somewhere along the way, I began to miss the mark. My time with Jesus did not affect my time with others. Church simply became a place for me to get my spiritual needs met, not to engage with the body of Christ. Even worse, I found myself despising other believers and easily noticing their faults.

The rise of individualistic spirituality began to flourish in the 16th century and has now become a mark of the western Christian. Our default way of thinking often makes it difficult to pursue unity among God's people, but our fellowship with other believers should be characterized by great love. This has not been the case for me, which is why Colossians 3:15-17 is so convicting. Verse 16 says, "Let the message about Christ, in all its richness, fill your lives." Let the gospel of Jesus fill you to the brim and empower you to live in community with others, loving and pursuing peace with them. The gospel is our starting point.

The Message version says it like this:
"Let the peace of Christ keep you in tune with each other, in step with each other. None of this going off and doing your own thing. And cultivate thankfulness. Let the Word of Christ—the Message—have the run of the house. Give it plenty of room in your lives. Instruct and direct one another using good common sense. And sing, sing your hearts out to God! Let every detail in your lives—words, actions, whatever—be done in the name of the Master, Jesus, thanking God the Father every step of the way."

Have you been living an isolated Christian life? You weren't meant to do this alone. God wants you to experience the full benefit of his family with all its quirks and hang-ups and oddities. Community isn't always easy, but it's the implication of following Jesus. When we decide to follow Immanuel, we are choosing to be with others just like he chose to be with us. How can you cultivate community today? Maybe it's a phone call, a note, or a batch of cookies. Maybe it's something more. Will you let the message of our incarnate God change the way you love others?

DAY
12

When He Makes Us Just

Proverbs 21:2-3

Reading

People may be right in their own eyes,
but the Lord examines their heart.
The Lord is more pleased when we do what is right and just
than when we offer him sacrifices.

Proverbs 21:2-3

Reflection

I have a confession: I'm a recovering Pharisee. I used to live by shoulds and oughts, and sometimes I still do. The thing about being a Pharisee is that it leaves little room for grace. Loving people gets pretty difficult when all your attention is focused on rules and regulations.

Proverbs 21:2-3 sounds like God cares more about love than he does about rules. He is more interested in the motivations of our hearts and how we're caring for other people. Not only that, doing justice will naturally flow from a heart that has been changed by grace. In his book, Generous Justice, pastor and author Tim Keller writes, "If a person has grasped the meaning of God's grace in his heart, he will do justice. If he doesn't live justly, then he may say with his lips that he is grateful for God's grace, but in his heart he is far from him. If he doesn't care about the poor, it reveals that at best he doesn't understand the grace he has experienced, and at worst he has not really encountered the saving mercy of God. Grace should make you just."

Proverbs 29:7 says, "The godly care about the rights of the poor; the wicked don't care at all." Doing justice is the natural result of falling in love with Jesus. Doing justice is the response to a God who rescued us when we were spiritually impoverished. We act justly because we know what it means to be in need.

Take the temperature of your heart. Have you been more concerned with following rules or loving people? Jesus came for people, not rules. Let's follow in his footsteps today. Is there someone in your life who needs to be loved well today? How can you make them feel seen?

When He Makes Us Generous

2 Corinthians 9:10-12

Reading

For God is the one who provides seed for the farmer and then bread to eat. In the same way, he will provide and increase your resources and then produce a great harvest of generosity in you. Yes, you will be enriched in every way so that you can always be generous. And when we take your gifts to those who need them, they will thank God. So two good things will result from this ministry of giving—the needs of the believers in Jerusalem will be met, and they will joyfully express their thanks to God.

2 Corinthians 9:10-12

Reflection

I'm not a worrier. That is, unless it comes to money. It has taken me years to trust that God will provide for my monetary needs and because of these financial fears, my heart is not prone to generosity. I'm stingy and tight-fisted, always concerned with saving up more cash just in case. You might as well call me Mrs. Scrooge. My husband, on the other hand, is always looking for an excuse to give. He wants to do it.

We like to talk about God being our Provider and how he is a good Father who wants to take care of his children. But what if there's another reason for his provision? 2 Corinthians 9:10 says he provides for us so that we will be generous. When he gives, we give. When he pours out, so do we. Because we can trust God to provide, we get to be joyfully generous.

I've learned to be generous over the years, but it took a while for my generosity to be joyful. I did it out of obligation at first because the Bible said to do it. Obligatory obedience always creates Pharisees, never disciples. It wasn't until I watched my husband being generous that my heart switched gears. 2 Corinthians 9:12 says that our generosity will result in two things: people's needs are met and God is glorified. My husband's joyful giving was motivated by those exact same things! His generosity wasn't a pharisaical chore, but rather a joyful response to the God who deserves to be praised.

Where is God calling you to be generous? Is it with your time or your finances? Maybe God wants you to be generously silent. For some of us, we struggle to listen well, so God might be calling us to give empathetic silence to someone else's pain. For others, we need to write a no-strings-attached check to a friend or family member. What has God given you that you can give to another?

When He Binds Us Together

Galatians 6:2-3

Reading

Share each other's burdens, and in this way obey the law of Christ. If you think you are too important to help someone, you are only fooling yourself.
You are not that important.

Galatians 6:2-3

Reflection

My mama always used to say, "Given the right circumstances, anyone is capable of doing anything." This was her way of trying to curb the pharisaical tendencies that had already begun to form in my childhood heart. I've been addicted to rules and guidelines, convinced that my adherence means I'm better than you.

That's when God knocks me off my self-made pedestal with passages like the one from today's reading. The burden-sharing life is contrary to pharisaical living. It's subversive in the face of self-reliance and it disrupts our pride. When speaking about the Pharisees, Jesus says in Matthew 23:4, "They crush people with unbearable religious demands and never lift a finger to ease the burden." Pharisees don't share burdens; they create them.

The writer of Galatians, the apostle Paul, knew this tension all too well. Before his conversion to Christianity, he was a Jewish rabbi who was famous for persecuting and killing followers of Jesus. He was a religious Jew who created burdens for Christians. Then he became a Christian himself, and the love of Jesus changed his life. So, when Paul writes in Galatians 6:2, "Share each other's burdens, and in this way obey the law of Christ," he is writing as a man who has been irrevocably changed.

When my mama cautioned, "Given the right circumstances, anyone is capable of doing anything," what she was really saying was this: the ground is level at the foot of the cross.

———————————

It would have been easy for me to latch onto the part of Galatians 6:2 that says, "and in this way obey the law of Christ." I wanted a rule to follow, but then I realized that the law of Christ is love. We obey love when we share burdens. Because of the love of God, we are compelled to care for each other. Is there someone in your life who needs help carrying a burden? How can you come alongside and ease their load?

———————————

When Communion Becomes
Our Calling

Luke 22:19-20

Reading

He took some bread and gave thanks to God for it. Then he broke it in pieces and gave it to the disciples, saying, "This is my body, which is given for you. Do this in remembrance of me." After supper he took another cup of wine and said, "This cup is the new covenant between God and his people—an agreement confirmed with my blood, which is poured out as a sacrifice for you.

Luke 22:19-20

Reflection

Dusk began to settle and the streets grew quiet. A holy calm engulfed the night as God's people took their familiar places at their familiar tables. The hustle and bustle of business was stilled—if only for a night—to remember. They took the Passover meal to remember how God rescued them from Egypt, how the blood of the lamb covered their doorposts, and how they were spared. But on this particular night, Jesus was going to start a new thing. This should come as no surprise to us now. Jesus is in the business of doing new things. He even tells us in Revelation 21:5, "See, I make all things new."

But this was going to be more than fresh perspective. Jesus was about to provide a radical calling for the people of God. Luke 22 says that Jesus took some bread, broke it, handed it out to the disciples, and said, "This is my body, which is given for you. Do this in remembrance of me."

Then he took a cup of wine and said, "This cup is the new covenant between God and his people—an agreement confirmed with my blood, which is poured out as a sacrifice for you." The Passover meal that once stood as a reminder of God's provision in Egypt would now be a reminder of Christ's sacrifice. Now we take the meal called communion to remember his body that was broken for us and his blood poured out on our behalf. But what if it's more than just remembrance? Jesus had a knack for object lessons, and I can't help but wonder if he's up to something in Luke 22.

In 1 Corinthians 11:24 we read Jesus's words, "This is my body, which is given for you. Do this to remember me." Then in 1 Corinthians 12:27 Paul says, "Now you are the body of Christ."

It's almost like Jesus is saying: *You are my body, broken and poured out for the world. Do this in remembrance of me.*

Jesus was using communion as an object lesson. He was showing us how to live as his followers. He was calling us to a life of brokenness that's poured out for others. We remember him by taking the sacred meal, yes, but also by replicating his actions in our day-to-day lives. We are the broken and poured out body of Christ. What does brokenness look like in your life lately? How has God used your brokenness to reveal himself to others?

DAY

16

When We Belong

Isaiah 43:1-2

Reading

But now, O Jacob, listen to the Lord who created you. O Israel, the one who formed you says, "Do not be afraid, for I have ransomed you. I have called you by name; you are mine. When you go through deep waters, I will be with you. When you go through rivers of difficulty, you will not drown. When you walk through the fire of oppression, you will not be burned up; the flames will not consume you.

Isaiah 43:1-2

Reflection

I didn't have many friends when I was a kid, especially at church. We moved around a lot and finally settled in a community when I was nine years old. By that point, most of the girls in my Sunday school class had known each other for years, and there was a clear bond of friendship that was withheld from newcomers like me. Add the fact that I was impossibly shy and odd, and loneliness became the obvious outcome. I remember being in Sunday school one week when the teacher asked if anyone could recite the memory verse. It was silent for a few seconds until I raised my hand and quoted Psalm 119:105, "Your word is a lamp to my feet and a light to my path." One of the other girls mumbled, "Show off," resulting in a wave of giggles from everyone else in the class. That day in Sunday school confirmed what I had already suspected to be true: I was an outsider.

Loneliness is a common weapon the enemy uses to convince us that we don't belong. This can make it easy to retreat from connection, both with God and others, and that's exactly what I did. The good news is that God is always in pursuit, even when we retreat. In the season of Advent, we acknowledge that he is our incarnate God. He is with us in our grief, in our loneliness, and in our pain. The Lord says in Isaiah 43:1, "'I have you called you by name; you are mine.'" When we don't feel like we belong anywhere else, we belong with him.

How has God been with you through difficult seasons? It's easier to trust God in the present when we remember his goodness in the past. Make a list of the ways he has cared for you. How does belonging to God change the way you approach other relationships?

When He Remembers

Isaiah 49:14-16

Reading

Yet Jerusalem says, "The Lord has deserted us; the Lord has forgotten us." "Never! Can a mother forget her nursing child? Can she feel no love for the child she has borne? But even if that were possible, I would not forget you! See, I have written your name on the palms of my hands.

Isaiah 49:14-16

Reflection

I'm a list maker. From grocery lists to housework lists to which bills need to be paid to projects at work to gift ideas for loved ones. My life would fall apart without writing things down because thoughts often leave my brain as soon as they're formed. I haven't always been like this though. It's a product of having too many things to remember and not enough space in my head. If you've ever forgotten something, it's not a great feeling, but forgetting a person feels even worse.

In Isaiah 49, God's people felt forgotten. They had been forcibly removed from their land and exiled to the pagan nation of Babylon. Separated from their homes and living as captives, they thought God had deserted them. But God isn't like me.

Today's reading likens God to a mother who cares for her young child. Her body longs to feed and nourish and sustain the child it created. God takes it a step further with his love for his people. He says that even if a mother could forget the child she birthed, he would not forget his people. He has even written your name on the palms of his hands, and not because he would otherwise forget you. Your name is on his hands because you reside in the center of his heart.

In the Old Testament, God is named El Roi, which means the God who sees me. God sees you in every season of your life. How does this truth change the way you approach your day?

When He Banishes Fear

Psalm 27:1-6

Reading

The Lord is my light and my salvation—
so why should I be afraid?
The Lord is my fortress, protecting me from danger,
so why should I tremble?
When evil people come to devour me,
when my enemies and foes attack me,
they will stumble and fall.
Though a mighty army surrounds me,
my heart will not be afraid.
Even if I am attacked,
I will remain confident.
The one thing I ask of the Lord—
the thing I seek most—
is to live in the house of the Lord all the days of my life,
delighting in the Lord's perfections
and meditating in his Temple.
For he will conceal me there when troubles come;
he will hide me in his sanctuary.
He will place me out of reach on a high rock.
Then I will hold my head high
above my enemies who surround me.
At his sanctuary I will offer sacrifices with shouts of joy,
singing and praising the Lord with music.

Psalm 27:1-6

Reflection

A few years ago, my husband and I visited our local zoo. We saw elephants and flamingos and tigers. We zig-zagged our way through the park with ease, completely calm and careless. That is, until we got to the reptiles. You see, I have a phobia of snakes. Simply looking at pictures of snakes sends me into a spiral complete with sweaty hands and a racing heart. On this particular day, my husband tried to help me overcome my fear by leading me into the reptile exhibit. I gave myself a pep talk and cautiously entered the cool, dark room. We made it about three steps inside before I burst into tears and ran back out.

Our fears aren't always logical, especially when faced with reality. The thing is, those snakes were trapped behind glass. They couldn't touch me! But my fear convinced me there was a real threat, and I panicked.

There are tons of other things that have the ability to hold our gaze and convince us that we're in danger, but if you're a child of God then you live in a reality that banishes fear. Psalm 27:5 says, "He will conceal me there when troubles come; he will hide me in his sanctuary. He will place me out of reach on a high rock." No danger can reach those who rest in his hands!

What makes you afraid? Read Psalm 27:1 again and record the reality of who God is in relation to your fears. How does this truth affect your life? How does Psalm 27:6 say we should respond in uncertainty?

When He Saves

Romans 5:6-8

Reading

When we were utterly helpless, Christ came at just the right time and died for us sinners. Now, most people would not be willing to die for an upright person, though someone might perhaps be willing to die for a person who is especially good. But God showed his great love for us by sending Christ to die for us while we were still sinners.

Romans 5:6-8

Reflection

No one likes to think of themselves as helpless. That's why the self-help industry makes billions of dollars every year! From books to television talk shows to podcasts, we want to know how to improve ourselves. But God said it's when we were utterly helpless that Jesus came to save us. This reveals the outrageous love of God. He saved us when we had nothing to give him in return, and he did it on purpose. When Jesus was challenged on his love for sinners in Mark 2, he responded in verse 17 by saying, "Healthy people don't need a doctor—sick people do." Jesus runs to the helpless. He runs to you.

This line of thinking is counterintuitive for me. I like to clean myself up to look presentable before I walk out into the world. I put my best foot forward in job interviews, downplaying my weaknesses and maximizing my strengths. I tidy my house before company comes over. Letting others see my mess is not an option. In fact, most of us would agree that it's downright irresponsible to let our messes be seen. But here's the tragic part: we can't come close to grasping the love of God until we embrace the mess. It is in our most vulnerable state that we find grace.

In his book Knowing God, J.I. Packer writes, "There is tremendous relief in knowing His love to me is utterly realistic, based at every point on prior knowledge of the worst about me, so that no discovery can disillusion him about me, in the way I am so often disillusioned about myself, and quench his determination to bless me." God knew everything you would ever do, and he still chose you. What does this reveal to you about the nature of God? What does this communicate about your value?

DAY
20

When He Empowers

Ephesians 3:16-19

Reading

I pray that from his glorious, unlimited resources he will empower you with inner strength through his Spirit. Then Christ will make his home in your hearts as you trust in him. Your roots will grow down into God's love and keep you strong. And may you have the power to understand, as all God's people should, how wide, how long, how high, and how deep his love is. May you experience the love of Christ, though it is too great to understand fully. Then you will be made complete with all the fullness of life and power that comes from God.

Ephesians 3:16-19

Reflection

A wise mentor once told me, "You can't pour out of an empty well." What she meant was that you can't love people effectively unless your personal love tank is full first. I remember her advice on days when I'm spent, irritable, and at the end of my rope. Those kinds of days happen more often than I'd like to admit.

Ephesians 3 says that God is the one who fills us up. He has unlimited resources to empower us with strength and overwhelm us with love. Your well won't run dry when you're planted in his love. It's tempting to plant ourselves in self-sufficiency, success, or people-pleasing, but those are superficial substitutes that won't hold out in the long run. When I'm feeling empty, that's a clear sign that my priorities have shifted.

Where are you planted? Ephesians 3:19 says that we will experience fullness of life and power when we plant ourselves with God. Think of a time when life felt full. How can you create space in your day to realign yourself with Jesus? He wants you to know the width and length and height and depth of his love, but first you have to be planted.

When He Makes a Way

Nehemiah 2:18-20

Reading

Then I told them about how the gracious hand of God had been on me, and about my conversation with the king. They replied at once, "Yes, let's rebuild the wall!" So they began the good work. But when Sanballat, Tobiah, and Geshem the Arab heard of our plan, they scoffed contemptuously. "What are you doing? Are you rebelling against the king?" they asked. I replied, "The God of heaven will help us succeed. We, his servants, will start rebuilding this wall. But you have no share, legal right, or historic claim in Jerusalem."

Nehemiah 2:18-20

———————

Reflection

God's people had returned from exile but the wall surrounding Jerusalem was in ruins. No wall meant they would be in constant danger of attack from surrounding enemies. No wall meant they were vulnerable to be conquered by yet another pagan nation. God's people weren't safe, but the task of rebuilding felt impossible. There was one man, however, who was burdened by the call to rebuild. His name was Nehemiah.

Nehemiah gathered the people and shared his vision to restore Jerusalem's wall. This is where our reading for today begins. God's people joined Nehemiah with great anticipation and excitement, eager for their home to be whole again. But shortly after they began, a few antagonistic men showed up to mock and jeer at the workers. A few verses earlier, these same men became very upset that Nehemiah had decided to lead the rebuilding effort because they wanted Jerusalem to remain vulnerable and open to outside attack.

Nehemiah responded without hesitation to their mockery. The God of heaven will help us succeed. Because he was secure in his calling, Nehemiah was able to be unwavering in his obedience. He was unmoved in the face of discouragement. And Nehemiah's dogged persistence resulted in an amazing feat. The wall around Jerusalem was completely rebuilt in just 52 days! The God of heaven did allow them to succeed.

Isaiah 61:4 tells us that we are all called to be rebuilders. We partner with Jesus in the work of rebuilding relationships, restoring peace, and reconciling communities. But the work of rebuilding will always be met with opposition. That's why we must be secure in our calling and unmoved in our obedience. How has God called you to participate in the work of rebuilding? Has the enemy tried to discourage you? What can you learn from Nehemiah's response in the midst of opposition?

DAY
22

When He is with Us

Psalm 16:5-8

Reading

Lord, you alone are my inheritance, my cup of blessing.

You guard all that is mine.

The land you have given me is a pleasant land.

What a wonderful inheritance!

I will bless the Lord who guides me;

even at night my heart instructs me.

I know the Lord is always with me.

I will not be shaken, for he is right beside me.

Psalm 16:5-8

Reflection

We all have the same desire: to be fully known and fully loved at the same time. This desire was placed inside of us all the way back in Genesis when God created us to be in relationship with him. His original intent was for pure, unadulterated love that would be untainted by shame. Sin pulls us away from God's intent, but he is constantly working to redeem our brokenness. He wants to be with us.

In Psalm 16, King David is praising the Lord for his faithful presence. Back in that day, a man's inheritance was reflected his value, so it's a big deal when David says in verse 5, "Lord, you alone are my inheritance." As the king over all of Israel, David doesn't care about material possessions or the praise of others. His heart pines for God alone. This would have been counter-cultural back then just as it is counter-cultural for us today. But when we read Psalm 16, we can't help but see God's redemption beginning to take hold. God's desire for restored, unashamed relationship is what we see reflected in today's reading. His chief longing is to be with us, and David writes in verse 8, "I know the Lord is always with me. I will not be shaken, for he is right beside me."

God knows you completely and loves you fully. All at once, he longs to be with you while knowing everything you've ever done. You are the object of his affection. Now that's radical love! King David of Israel was a man who yearned for the presence of God. What does your heart yearn for? How can you be attentive to God's presence today?

When He is Enough

Psalm 23

Reading

The Lord is my shepherd; I have all that I need. He lets me rest in green meadows; he leads me beside peaceful streams. He renews my strength. He guides me along right paths bringing honor to his name. Even when I walk through the darkest valley, I will not be afraid, for you are close beside me. Your rod and your staff protect and comfort me. You prepare a feast for me in the presence of my enemies. You honor me by anointing my head with oil. My cup overflows with blessings. Surely your goodness and unfailing love will pursue me all the days of my life, and I will live in the house of the Lord forever.

Psalm 23

Reflection

The holidays tend to make me feel frantic. From buying gifts for loved ones to festive parties to family gatherings, it's all a little much for this introvert. If I'm not careful, it's easy to prioritize busyness over rest. That's why Psalm 23 is so comforting. It realigns my heart with the truth that the Lord is all I need. He has already given me the thing my soul longs for—peace.

He offers strength when we're spent, guidance when we're lost, protection from our enemy, and provision in scarcity. We lack nothing because we have him. In a season that begs us to spend more, do more, and be more, God simply wants us to be with him. The descriptions listed in Psalm 23 all depend on one factor—we must be with the Shepherd in order to experience these benefits. The end of the chapter is the best part. He isn't just waiting to be with us; he is actively pursuing. Verse 6 says, "Surely your goodness and unfailing love will pursue me all the days of my life." He won't stop reaching out and moving in your direction.

Do a heart check. Where is your focus today? Will you choose your checklist or your Shepherd? Take some time to rest in his presence today. Look for the ways he has been in pursuit of your heart.

When He Rules

Isaiah 9:6-7

Reading

For a child is born to us, a son is given to us.
The government will rest on his shoulders.
And he will be called:
Wonderful Counselor, Mighty God,
Everlasting Father, Prince of Peace.
His government and its peace will never end.
He will rule with fairness and justice from the throne of
his ancestor David for all eternity.
The passionate commitment of the Lord of Heaven's
Armies will make this happen!

Isaiah 9:6-7

———————————

Reflection

In a world full of chaos, injustice, and uncertainty, God knew exactly what we needed—a Messiah. We needed someone to set things right, someone to rescue us from ourselves, and someone who would rule with might. That person is Jesus. If we ever wonder where God is in the middle of this messy world, the answer always lies in Jesus. Today's reading tells us exactly what we got when Jesus erupted into our realm: Wonderful Counselor, Mighty God, Everlasting Father, Prince of Peace. These are names but they're also job descriptions. He will be these things for us.

There are many variables in my life that have the potential to overwhelm me. I'm bombarded by deadlines, immersed in adult decisions, and faced with broken relationships. There is one factor that keeps the panic at bay: Jesus rules it all. He is in charge! Because he is over everything, I can loosen my white-knuckled grip of control and trust him to be who Isaiah 9:6-7 says he is. Saving the world isn't my job, and that's the best news for a perfectionist like me.

Jesus reigns over everything, even the parts of your life that feel too big. He reigns over grief, over pain, over difficult decisions, over doubt, and over fear. What in your life feels too big for God? Which of the descriptions in today's reading is the most difficult for you to believe about Jesus? Pray that the Lord would make himself known to you in a fresh way today.

When He was Born

Luke 2:1-15

Reading

At that time the Roman emperor, Augustus, decreed that a census should be taken throughout the Roman Empire. This was the first census taken when Quirinius was governor of Syria.) All returned to their own ancestral towns to register for this census. And because Joseph was a descendant of King David, he had to go to Bethlehem in Judea, David's ancient home. He traveled there from the village of Nazareth in Galilee. He took with him Mary, to whom he was engaged, who was now expecting a child. And while they were there, the time came for her baby to be born. She gave birth to her firstborn son. She wrapped him snugly in strips of cloth and laid him in a manger, because there was no lodging available for them. That night there were shepherds staying in the fields nearby, guarding their flocks of sheep. Suddenly, an angel of the Lord appeared among them, and the radiance of the Lord's glory surrounded them. They were terrified, but the angel reassured them. "Don't be afraid!" he said. "I bring you good news that will bring great joy to all people. The Savior—yes, the Messiah, the Lord—has been born today in Bethlehem, the city of David! And you will recognize him by this sign: You will find a baby wrapped snugly in strips of cloth, lying in a manger." Suddenly, the angel was joined by a vast host of others—the armies of heaven—praising God and saying, "Glory to God in highest heaven, and peace on earth to those with whom God is pleased." When the angels had returned to heaven, the shepherds said to each other, "Let's go to Bethlehem! Let's see this thing that has happened, which the Lord has told us about."

Luke 2:1-15

Reflection

On the greatest night in history, a quiet reverence swept over the earth. Our mighty Jesus was born in humility with little fanfare or recognition. The birth of a king had never happened like this before and never would again. One thing is undeniable: when people heard about Jesus, they couldn't stay away. The shepherds left their fields and the livestock that was their livelihood, all for Jesus. His presence changed everything.

His birth began a new chapter for all of us. Because of Jesus, life with God would now be characterized by hope and peace and joy. His presence signaled grace for a messed up world. Immanuel was God's ultimate rescue plan to restore relationship with us.

There is fullness of joy in his presence. What can you learn from the shepherds' response to the birth of Jesus? Take some time today to reflect on his nearness and bask in his peace. May you be filled with the joy that only his presence can bring.

Joy to the World
Isaac Watts

Joy to the world, the Lord is come! Let earth re-ceive her King____ Let

e - very - heart____ pre - pare Him room____ And Heaven and na - ture sing and

Heaven and na - ture sing and Hea - ven and Hea - ven and na - ture sing.

Joy to the world, the Savior reigns
Let men their songs employ
While fields and floods
Rocks, hills and plains
Repeat the sounding joy
Repeat the sounding joy
Repeat, repeat, the sounding joy

Joy to the world, the Lord is come
Let earth receive her King
Let every heart
Prepare Him room
And heaven and nature sing
And heaven and nature sing
And heaven and heaven and nature sing

CPSIA information can be obtained
at www.ICGtesting.com
Printed in the USA
LVHW01s2047231117
557350LV00009B/65/P